D1445732

# Samuel Adams

## Discover the Life of a Colonial American

Kieran Walsh

Rourke

Publishing LLC
Vero Beach, Florida 32964

www.rourkepublishing.com

PHOTO CREDITS: Cover and page 21 ©Getty Images; title, pp 15, 16 from the Library of Congress; All other photos ©North Wind Picture Archives

Title Page: *A scene of a Revolutionary War battle*

Editor: Frank Sloan

Cover and page design by Nicola Stratford

**Library of Congress Cataloging-in-Publication Data**

Walsh, Kieran.
  Samuel Adams / Kieran Walsh.
    p. cm. -- (Discover the life of a colonial American)
  Includes bibliographical references and index.
  ISBN 1-59515-135-4
  1. Adams, Samuel, 1722-1803--Juvenile literature. 2. Politicians--United States--Biography--Juvenile literature. 3. United States. Declaration of Independence--Signers--Biography--Juvenile literature. 4. United States--History--Revolution, 1775-1783--Biography--Juvenile literature. I. Title. II. Series: Walsh, Kieran. Discover the life of a colonial American.
  E302.6.A2W35 2004
  973.3'092--dc22
                              2004009652

Printed in the USA

CG/CG

# Table of Contents

# A Young Student

Samuel Adams was born on September 27, 1722 in Boston, Massachusetts. As a young man, Adams attended Harvard University, where he read the works of John Locke, an English philosopher. Locke believed strongly in religious freedom, the right to own property, and the pursuit of happiness. These ideas had a great influence on Samuel Adams.

*Harvard as it looked during the time Samuel Adams went to school there.*

# Colonies under British Rule

Though Adams studied law at Harvard, he found himself drawn to another pursuit after graduating. A fiery speaker with **radical** views, Adams quickly made a name for himself in Massachusetts politics. Eventually he was elected to the Massachusetts legislature in 1765.

**At this** time, the American colonies were still under British rule. In order to raise money from the colonies, the British government had imposed a number of expensive taxes.

*Samuel Adams sits looking at a wall map.*

# The Stamp Act

One of these was the Stamp Act. It charged a tax on printed goods like newspapers, advertisements, and pamphlets.

Many colonists, including Samuel Adams, felt the Stamp Act was unfair. In 1765, Adams helped found the Sons of Liberty, a group that fought the Stamp Act by refusing to buy British goods—a method of protest called **boycotting**.

The Stamp Act was **repealed** in 1766. In 1767, though, the Townshend Acts introduced new taxes on items like paints, glass, and tea.

*Colonial citizens protest the Stamp Act.*

# "Taxation without Representation"

In 1768 Adams wrote a **Circular** Letter—a letter that was sent to each of the 13 American colonies. The letter explained to people why they had to oppose the British government and fight all forms of "taxation without **representation**."

**Resistance** to British taxes and British rule grew. To enforce the taxes, the British government sent more troops to the colonies.

*British troops enter Boston.*

# The Boston Massacre

In 1770, tensions between the soldiers and the colonists exploded when the British troops began firing at a mob. During this event, now known as the Boston Massacre, five people were killed.

*British soldiers open fire in the Boston Massacre.*

*Samuel Adams warns the British governor after the Boston Massacre.*

# The Boston Tea Party

All of the Townshend Acts were repealed in 1770, except the tax on tea.

In 1773, three British ships carrying tea arrived in Boston. Governor Thomas Hutchinson refused to let the ships leave until the people of Boston paid the tea tax. On December 16, 1773, a group of men inspired by Samuel Adams snuck aboard the ships and dumped the tea into the harbor. This event has since become known as the Boston Tea Party.

*Colonials dressed as Native Americans dump tea in Boston harbor.*

# The Continental Congress

In 1774, Samuel Adams joined a group of **representatives** from the 13 colonies. The group was called the Continental Congress. The Congress was formed in order to solve the problems the colonists were having with Britain.

*Delegates leave Independence Hall after signing the Declaration of Independence.*

Unlike Samuel Adams, some members of the Congress wanted the colonies to remain part of Britain. By 1775, a reunion with the Britain looked impossible.

In 1776, Samuel Adams was one of the members of the Congress who signed the Declaration of Independence. This document declared that the United States was separate from Britain.

*Delegates sign the Declaration of Independence.*

# The Revolutionary War

   The Revolutionary War began in 1775 with the battle at Lexington, Massachusetts. The war lasted until October 1781 when the British army surrendered at Yorktown. In 1783, the Treaty of Paris recognized the United States as a new nation.

   When the Revolutionary War was over, Samuel Adams left the Continental Congress. It was not the end of Adams's political career, though. Between 1789 and 1794 he served as lieutenant governor of Massachusetts and later as governor of Massachusetts from 1794 to 1797.

*The British surrender in Yorktown ended the Revolutionary War.*

# A Great Patriot

After retiring in 1797, Samuel Adams lived in Boston until his death in 1803.

Without Samuel Adams, it is possible that the American Revolution might never have happened. A brilliant writer and speaker, Adams used his gifts to urge his fellow colonists to fight for their rights.

*Samuel Adams was a good writer and speaker.*

# Important Dates to Remember

| | |
|---|---|
| 1722 | Born in Boston, Massachusetts |
| 1765 | Elected to the Massachusetts legislature |
| 1765 | Founds the Sons of Liberty |
| 1773 | The Boston Tea Party |
| 1774 | Adams joins the Continental Congress |
| 1776 | Adams signs the Declaration of Independence |
| 1789-1794 | Serves as lieutenant governor of Massachusetts |
| 1794-1797 | Serves as governor of Massachusetts |
| 1803 | Dies in Boston |

# Glossary

**boycotting** (BOI kott ing) — a form of protest that involves the refusal to buy or use certain goods

**circular** (SER kyuh lur) — sent to a large number of people

**legislature** (LEG uh SLAY chur) — a government body that makes laws

**radical** (RAD ih kul) — unusual or extreme

**repealed** (ree PEELD) — taken out of existence; removed

**representation** (REP rih ZEN tay shun) — having a vote in the decision-making process

**representatives** (REP rih ZENT ut ivz) — members of a government body

**resistance** (rih ZIS tunts) — opposition

# Index

## Further Reading

Fradin, Dennis Brindell. *Samuel Adams: The Father of American Independence*.
Clarion Books, 1998

Freedman, Russell. *Give Me Liberty: The Story of the Declaration of Independence*.
Holiday House, 2000

Irvin, Benjamin. *Samuel Adams: Son of Liberty, Father of Revolution*. Oxford University
Press, 2002

Stefoff, Rebecca. *American Revolution: 1700-1800*. Benchmark Books, 2001

## Websites to Visit

http://www.infoplease.com/ce6/people/A0802441.html, Infoplease – Samuel Adams
http://encarta.msn.com/encyclopedia_761569134/Samuel_Adams.html
Microsoft Encarta Encyclopedia Article – Samuel Adams
http://www.patriotresource.com/people/samadams.html
The Patriot Resource – Samuel Adams

## About the Author

Kieran Walsh is a writer of children's nonfiction books, primarily on historical and
social studies topics. Walsh has been involved in the children's book field as editor,
proofreader, and illustrator as well as author.